**Inside
the Blood Factory**

Books by Diane Wakoski

INSIDE THE BLOOD FACTORY
THE GEORGE WASHINGTON POEMS (*Riverrun Press*)
DISCREPANCIES AND APPARITIONS

Inside
the Blood Factory

Diane Wakoski

1968
Doubleday & Company, Inc., Garden City, New York

LIBRARY OF CONGRESS CATALOG CARD NUMBER 68–27104
COPYRIGHT © 1962, 1968 BY DIANE WAKOSKI
ALL RIGHTS RESERVED
PRINTED IN THE UNITED STATES OF AMERICA
FIRST EDITION

Contents

I. Blue Monday

II. Poems to The Man in the Silver Ferrari

III. From The Tarot Deck

IV. The Ice Eagle

I

Blue Monday

Blue Monday

Blue of the heaps of beads poured into her breasts
and clacking together in her elbows;
blue of the silk
that covers lily-town at night;
blue of her teeth
that bite cold toast
and shatter on the streets;
blue of the dyed flower petals with gold stamens
hanging like tongues
over the fence of her dress
at the opera/ opals clasped under her lips
and the moon breaking over her head a
gush of blood-red lizards.

Blue Monday. Monday at 3:00 and
Monday at 5. Monday at 7:30 and
Monday at 10:00. Monday passed under the rippling
California fountain. Monday alone
a shark in the cold blue waters.

>   You are dead: wound round like a paisley shawl.
>   I cannot shake you out of the sheets. Your name
>   is still wedged in every corner of the sofa.

>   Monday is the first of the week,
>   and I think of you all week.
>   I beg Monday not to come
>   so that I will not think of you
>   all week.

You paint my body blue. On the balcony
in the soft muddy night, you paint me
with bat wings and the crystal
the crystal
the crystal
the crystal in your arm cuts away
the night, folds back ebony whale skin
and my face, the blue of new rifles,
and my neck, the blue of Egypt,
and my breasts, the blue of sand,
and my arms, bass-blue,
and my stomach, arsenic;

there is electricity dripping from me like cream;
there is love dripping from me I cannot use—like acacia or
jacaranda—fallen blue and gold flowers, crushed into the street.

          Love passed me in a blue business suit
          and fedora.
          His glass cane, hollow and filled with
          sharks and whales . . .
          He wore black
          patent leather shoes
          and had a mustache. His hair was so black
          it was almost blue.

          "Love," I said.
          "I beg your pardon," he said.
          "Mr. Love," I said.
          "I beg your pardon," he said.

          So I saw there was no use bothering him on the street

          Love passed me on the street in a blue
          business suit. He was a banker
          I could tell.

So blue trains rush by in my sleep.
Blue herons fly overhead.
Blue paint cracks in my
arteries and sends titanium
floating into my bones.
Blue liquid pours down
my poisoned throat and blue veins
rip open my breast. Blue daggers tip
and are juggled on my palms.
Blue death lives in my fingernails.

If I could sing one last song
with water bubbling through my lips
I would sing with my throat torn open,
the blue jugular spouting that black shadow pulse,
and on my lips
I would balance volcanic rock
emptied out of my veins. At last
my children strained out
of my body. At last my blood
solidified and tumbling into the ocean.
It is blue.
It is blue.
It is blue.

The Night A Sailor Came to Me in a Dream

At the point of shining feathers,
that moment when dawn
ran her finger along the knife edge sky;
at the point when chickens come out of the living room rug
to peck for corn and the grains like
old yellow eyes
roll as marbles across the floor;
at that sweet sprouting point when the seed of day
rests on your tongue,
and you haven't swallowed reality yet. Then,
then, yes, at that instant of shimmering new pine needles
came a dream, a blister from a new burn,
and you walked in,
old times,
no player piano or beer,
reality held my toes,
the silver ball of sleep was on my stomach,
the structure of dream,
like a harness
lowered over my head, around me,
and I cannot remember what you said, though the harbor was foggy,
and your pea coat seemed to drip with moisture.

Thirty years of travelling this ocean.

Perhaps you told me
you were not
dead.

Sestina from the Home Gardener

These dried-out paint brushes which fell from my lips have been removed
with your departure; they are such minute losses
compared with the light bulb gone from my brain, the sections
of chicken wire from my liver, the precise
silver hammers in my ankles which delicately banged and pointed
magnetically to you. Love has become unfamiliar

and plenty of time to tend the paint brushes now. Once unfamiliar
with my processes. Once removed
from that sizzling sun, the ego, to burn my poet shadow to the wall,
I pointed,
I suppose, only to your own losses
which made you hate that 200 pound fish called marriage. Precise
ly, I hate my life, hate its freedom, hate the sections

of fence stripped away, hate the time for endless painting, hate the
sections
of my darkened brain that wait for children to snap on the light, the
unfamiliar
corridors of my heart with strangers running in them, shouting. The
precise
incisions in my hip to extract an image, a dripping pickaxe or palmtree
removed
and each day my paint brushes get softer and cleaner—better tools, and
losses
cease to mean loss. Beauty, to each eye, differently pointed.

I admire sign painters and carpenters. I like that black hand pointed
up a drive-way whispering to me, "The Washingtons live in those
    sections"
and I explain autobiographically that George Washington is sympathetic
    to my losses;
His face or name is everywhere. No one is unfamiliar
with the American dollar, and since you've been removed
from my life I can think of nothing else. A precise

replacement for love can't be found. But art and money are precise
ly for distraction. The stars popping out of my blood are pointed
nowhere. I have removed
my ankles so that I cannot travel. There are sections
of my brain growing teeth and unfamiliar
hands tie strings through my eyes. But there are losses

Of the spirit like vanished bicycle tires and losses
of the body, like the whole bike, every precise
bearing, spoke, gear, even the unfamiliar
handbrakes vanished. I have pointed
myself in every direction, tried sections
of every map. It's no use. The real body has been removed.

Removed by the ice tongs. If a puddle remains what losses
can those sections of glacier be? Perhaps a precise
count of drops will substitute the pointed mountain, far away, un-
    familiar?

Rain Trip

You spot me in the rain journey
walking the road strewn with fish bones;
from your railroad car you see me disappearing
like sugar
in water.
What is your substance, she asks me every day.
        iron that rusts in the rain
        flower lips with moisture-charged membranes
        glass that washes clean in the water
        silk that squeaks & crushes & stains in the ocean—
        the water-mark
        sand that swirls and changes places
        a groundhog who shakes his quills
but I cannot give her one answer.

Your name is the formula I keep in labyrinths.
Medicine bottles under my bed hold your fingers.
Naked, I am a tree gypsy: you can't shake me out of your branches.
This accuser tries to flake me. Love sits at the root of my tongue
and will not walk with me.
She does not know
or cannot accept
my longing for you who pass through my life without even iodine traces.
Inspect my blood. Tell her you have shaken the letters from the
alphabet and left an
incomplete
world.

The Father of My Country

All fathers in Western civilization must have
a military origin. The
ruler,
governor,
yes,
he is
was the
general at one time or other.
And George Washington
won the hearts
of his country—the rough military man
with awkward
sincere
drawing-room manners.

My father;
have you ever heard me speak of him? I seldom
do. But I had a father,
and he had military origins—or my origins from
him
are military,
militant. That is, I remember him only in uniform. But of the navy,
30 years a chief petty officer,
Always away from home.

It is rough/hard for me to
speak now.

16

I'm not used to talking
about him.
Not used to
naming his objects/
objects
that never surrounded me.

A woodpecker with fresh bloody crest
knocks
at my mouth. Father, for the first
time I say
your name. Name rolled in thick Polish parchment scrolls,
name of Roman candle drippings when I sit at my table
alone, each night,
name of naval uniforms and name of
telegrams, name of
coming home from your aircraft carrier,
name of shiny shoes,
name of Hawaiian dolls, name
of mess spoons, name of greasy machinery, and name of
stencilled names.
Is it your blood I carry in a test tube,
my arm,
to let fall, crack, and spill on the sidewalk
in front of the men
I know,
I love,
I know, and
want? So you left my house when I was under two,
being replaced by other machinery, and
I didn't believe you left me.

          This scene: the trunk yielding treasures of
          a green fountain pen, heart-shaped mirror,
          amber beads, old letters with brown ink, and
          the gopher snake stretched across the palm tree

in the front yard with woody trunk like monkey skins,
and a sunset through the skinny persimmon trees. You
came walking, not even a telegram or post card from
Tahiti. Love, love, through my heart like ink in
the thickest nubbed pen, black and flowing into words.
You came to me, and I at least six. Six doilies
of lace, six battleship cannon, six old beerbottles,
six thick steaks, six love letters, six clocks running
backwards, six watermelons, and six baby teeth, a six
cornered hat on six men's heads, six lovers at once
or one lover at sixes and sevens; how I confuse
all this with my
dream
walking the tightrope bridge
with gold knots
over
the mouth of an anemone/ tissue spiral lips
and holding on so that the ropes burned
as if my wrists had been tied

If George Washington
had not
been the Father
of my Country,
it is doubtful that I would ever have
found
a father. Father in my mouth, on my lips, in my
tongue, out of all my womanly fire,
Father I have left in my steel filing cabinet as a name on my birth
certificate, Father, I have left in the teeth pulled out at
dentists' offices and thrown into their garbage cans,
Father living in my wide cheekbones and short feet,
Father in my Polish tantrums and my American speech, Father, not a
holy name, not a name I cherish but the name I bear, the name
that makes me one of a kind in any phone book because
you changed it, and nobody

18

but us
has it,
Father who makes me dream in the dead of night of the falling cherry
blossoms, Father who makes me know all men will leave me
if I love them,
Father who made me a maverick,
a writer
a namer,
name/father, sun/father, moon/father, bloody mars/father,

other children said, "My father is a doctor,"
or
"My father gave me this camera,"
or
"My father took me to
the movies,"
or
"My father and I went swimming,"
but
my father is coming in a letter
once a month
for a while,
and my father
sometimes came in a telegram
but
mostly
my father came to me
in sleep, my father because I dreamed in one night that I dug through
the ash heap in back of the pepper tree and found a diamond shaped like
a dog and my father called the dog and it came leaping over to him and
he walked away out of the yard down the road with the dog jumping
and yipping at his heels,

my father was not in the telephone book
in my city;
my father was not sleeping with my mother

at home;
my father did not care if I studied the
piano;
my father did not care what
I did;
and I thought my father was handsome and I loved him and I wondered
why
he left me alone so much,
so many years
in fact, but
my father
made me what I am
a lonely woman
without a purpose, just as I was
a lonely child
without any father. I walked with words, words, and names,
names. Father was not
one of my words.
Father was not
one of my names. But now I say, George you have become my father,
in his 20th century naval uniform. George Washington, I need your
love; George, I want to call you Father, Father, my Father,
Father of my country,
that is
me. And I say the name to chant it. To sing it. To lace it around me
like weaving cloth. Like a happy child on that shining afternoon in
the palmtree sunset with her mother's trunk yielding treasures,
I cry and
cry,
Father,
Father,
Father,
have you really come home?

The House of the Heart

My shoes are suede boxes
clomping down the corridors to Nut,
Egyptian,
tall, long-toed lady of the night with the zodiac
in her belly.
Inside my head the serpent has slithered
under my deep comfortable bed; I dream to offset
my empty brain. The sun is being born
with shaky legs, slender as new beans,
and my music is the same old sad tune,
the house of the heart
where the heart lives,
where it lies at night
in its warm saucer of blood; the house of the heart
always welcomes visitors from the moon,
some from the sun
if they take off their shoes.

My shoes carry me heavily
translating my bones into words,
carrying the blood in envelopes to the post office
to mail to the world. Deep under now
with spices in my nose,
silk wrapped around my heart so that it will not wither
before Truth weighs it on her scale.
My shoes have come with me all this way,
this journey through the beetle kingdom
—larvae are licking the cake from my fingers,

cake I last fed to the ducks by the river,
their green heads shining into the palms of my hands like oiled nuts,
their bills ready to scratch the words on my heart which would
give it sacred content and help it on Truth's scales.
My shoes with their clumsy square toes
hold my clumsy feet. They have walked,
never danced, walked everywhere for me.

Sun, come into the house of my heart.
Take off your burning shoes. Don't let them touch
even my doorstep. Their flame would burn far down
even below my passageway.

Moon, come into the house of my heart.
Take off your shoes. Knock on the door with a silver ring.
Pass over the lintel as a lichee nut would roll down my throat.
Come down the dark passageway with a candle, with a silver
light, with a drop of hot oil of peppermint on your cool
tongue. Moon, walk in. Come in. But your silvery shoes
must be left outside the door
to the house of my heart.

Water Shapes

Everywhere
this pool is a giant black bug,
trying to climb into my mouth and steal away
every message written on my teeth;
my tongue,
like a pen that writes under water
frantically demonstrating a languageless
script,
tries to talk
has nothing to say
                  A knife that tries to take
away my breath. Blood, too,
like ink or water,
writes messages
saying
this water is filled with scorpions &
water skimmers—their legs like the threads of your hair
left on the pillow in the morning. The sleep
in your neck, breathing, a light on a pool

I watch you sleep
in the anger of my own hair,
which is long
        and wants to tie knots,
strangle, avenge this face of mine
which is the water of the Southern Arctic seas
and has been drowned
swollen out of shape.

One message is written in the pulse,
another in the sleeping face;
always I am asking the water to be fire,
to shine like lights,
to burn in the night,
even when there is no explanation
for such a transformation.

Sleep Incantation

I don't want to die though my teeth are cut off at the gum
and clink together like seashells
in the beach bag;

I don't want destruction—
black hair tangled around my strangling throat,
razors splitting open the vein seams,
or poisons
stiffening the rubbery muscles;

I want sleep. Sleep to dream
of the four child bodies
in white winding sheets,
my Egyptian heritage turning up and floating through
my blood stream like light bulbs
the filaments connecting with
my brain, shiny black
bulls walking
heavy-hoofed over my arms,
down my back, under my
neck. Sleep is
the delicate tread of chickens. Sleep
slants its way into my
fingers. Sleet, icy and wet
comes out of my hands and
slaps a dream to the ground.

2

The dream runs away with a little
yowl. The cold wet
razor we all distrust
seduces my eyelid. Sleep
comes. I want sleep to knot
me to the dental chair. I
want sleep to water me
like begonias. I want
sleep as smooth as banana
skins and as sweet as sugar
on the rim of an icy glass.

Pour me into sleep. I can find
only one
delicate
displacement of
love;
yet it has
pulled all my muscles
diagonal
and now I need sleep,
need to surrender to the strong arms,
those arms I do not
love.
I sleep because the love flower has rotted in my mouth
and trickles its black liquid, like a poison mushroom
down my throat.

In Gratitude To Beethoven

The full roses with all their petals like the wrinkles of laughter
on your face as you bend to kiss someone
are bursting on the bush,
spotting my arm, as I carry a bundle of them
to my friends;
they seem to have come out of my skin
on this hot fragrant night,
and I imagine the inside of my body
glowing, phosphorescent, with strange flower faces
looking out from the duodenum
or the soft liver,
white as my belly, the eyes always disbelieving
the ugly processes that make a living body.

Here I am,
admittedly a strange combination of images;
yet constantly myself,
a funny series of animals
from the grey field mouse quietly stealing through the grain
caught by the silvery gopher snake sleekly sliding
across the grass,
caught and lifted, wriggling like a wild muscle trying to free itself
by the fierce open-eyed hawk,
being bitten itself by the deceptively soft tiger who will eat
    strange meat,
and is shot by the man, the hunter,
who kills for sport. Somewhere there is a consistency,
perhaps the thread of destruction,

making me a predator in every cycle
except the first one,
and I have travelled so far away from my beginnings;
no one loves me:
That I can say with certainty,
without fear of contradiction in a hundred years,
by the series of images passing,
and of course I am always
slipping through life
alone
as I am tonight,
feeling especial gratitude for Beethoven
who, in spite of all fashions,
remains a companion, whose place no one can take
permanently.
His music
has all the life you loving people I hate so much
are trying to squeeze out of me.

Yesterday I discovered I was a stingy person;
today that even my gratitudes come out of angers
at others. Who would admit as much
about himself, that he was such a failure
at creating that ultimate human good—love.

Let me say it publicly, as openly as I can,
with no delicacy or tact:
I am like the guerilla fighter
who must sleep with one eye open for attack, a knife
or poison, a bamboo dart could come at any time.

No one has loved me without trying to destroy me,
there is no part of me that is not armoured,
there is no moment when I am not expecting attack,
there is no one I trust,
there is no love left in me that is not a wild flower,

growing at its own leisure with no cultivation period and no sense
of order;
one, perhaps, that only Beethoven,
now a violin or harp or piano,
could love.

At times, like now,
I am filled with the anger of bitterness,
a sense of having been betrayed
and then cling even more fervently to old Ludwig
whose sonatas I played for so many years
feeling
the field mouse in me slipping out through the pores in my skin,
running about the dusty grain field,
looking for food.
Sometimes I see my life as a cancer,
a growth with no purpose,
one that got out of hand, by some malfunctioning organ.

At times, you who look at me with so much tenderness,
you make me cry.
Where are you when I need you?
This is all literary invention, a way of
talking when there is no life.
Must it be the reality?
No one has ever moved more than the surfaces,
the images. Where is reverence
for the dialogue,
the process?
One friend tells me in the super market that I'm a bourgeois housewife
and won't speak to me for three hours, after my mentioning a
need for protein; another tells me I'm a
pushy little girl
after a conversation in which there was no agreement;
another says I'm a bad philosopher;
and another that I'm weak because I cling to a man who can destroy me;

but most friends tell me nothing,
are simply not there when I need them.
It is their way of dealing with the proliferation of images.

Beethoven, my gratitude for you
knows no limitations.
I keep looking for a man who will satisfactorily replace you
in my life.
That would seem to show no gratitude,
no satisfaction.
It is
in fact
only a music I have
in my ears.
A need for a similar richness.

II

Poems to The Man
in the Silver Ferrari

This King: The Tombed Egyptian One

deep in his coiled eyes
under the lids
mosaicked with images of beach plums
holding his own in the fire
that burns across the ocean at 3:00
there is a hammer that
taps hello and good-bye to each
word and sound.

Oh song of the sun
oh apricot arms and palms scattered on the
drying trays
oh textures of water under the
glass of the skin
oh waves that wash past my ears and stiffen me,
that keep you in your magnificent sepulchre
and keep me from you by humming-bird wings,
oh the antique desperation of our
lives.
I want to smash through the fortified walls of myself
with a sledge
I want to rescue the swallows' nest in your
unlit halls.

To The Man in the Silver Ferrari
a journal

Monday

of the moon in my throat
asking you
to come
to touch it
touch my throat

the airplane hovers over this map
the boat lingers out just beyond
the harbor,
where are you/ just beyond the cliff?
my body,
just beyond the trees,
they grow in the water, their branches move like
porpoises; they are cuttlefish at night;
where are you? just inside my shadow,
the cranes whistle at dawn
I check the shore to see if you've been here,
find only a few feathers/
not the right kind/ . . .

my body lives in the salt shaker.
they have packed me in,
thinking I was a grain of rice.

today, early this morning,
I took the train—wanting to play Anna Karenina but refraining—

to the seashore where I am now,
thinking of you, a lover with a mustache,
who is also not here,
who is also with someone else, somewhere else,
who also, who also,
who also, who also,
what else can I say? Else is there any meaning to life.
or else there isn't. or else something else is meant else where
in another time/
the mushrooms are everywhere out here, growing from the haystack
and under the trees, in the meadow, and by the porch—
different kinds. I wonder what mushrooms you are eating
or dreaming of or seeing
wherever you are now. I miss your mustache,
have always wished George Washington had a mustache.

The morning glory is 100 sapphires,
it is a moon flower,
it waits for the water to moisten its lips,
it waits for the rough wooden fence,
it falls in my ears at night,
it grows in your mustache,
it wraps my body in its one booming flower.
By the moon we are connected,
moons hang from the morning glory vine—white squash,
the chords tie us together:
it is sound that ties us together.

I hear you. I hear you,
if you would only talk.

Come back,
and bring me
a new moon.

Tuesday

Mars, they say,
is red,
in the sky,
though such distinctions
as red or blue
or steady or twinkling I cannot
discern. My eye not having
the subtleties
of my heart;
or my tongue. Likewise.
Yet my subtle heart looks for canals
and signs of life
in you, your planet, your body, your universe; is it a galaxy?
Today I did battle with huge black-green flies
that sucked at me in the sun along the shore
leaving yellow lumps under my tanning legs.
And I thought of you
often, as I have each night and day since you've been gone.

Whisper to me in my ear, you said,
and the candle of my mouth melted into your ear
swimming with bloody love knots. I think
oftener when you're gone.
I marvel to get through another day
and know there are days and days more to come.
We parcel them out. Five days here, a month there,
a year doing this, a few days doing that,
hoping somehow the burden of days will not seem so long.
Mars, they say, is the knife, is the
cut-throat,
bringing blood instead of words.
Mars, I cannot tell you from the others
when you are in the sky.

36

Someday, I will see you walking along the street with your
bloody knife, and dread you.
All those subtle knives which have delicately chopped
inside my veins this lifetime
have to be washed, dried, and put away.
This Mars day, I miss you,
cannot find you
in the sky.

Wednesday

Quicksilver, the day on the waters,
delving into the silt
for quickly scudding clams, burrowing their way into
the bay.
Mercury, the patron of Virgo, and Gemini, bestows this day
with strange fast patterns,
dips ideas into my brain pan like dunking toast in coffee.
And the deep coffee mud sucks
her clams sweetly,
deeply, dunking them into her belly.
Where are you today? The same place you were yesterday,
and the day before?

My thoughts turn over like a patchwork quilt.
My feelings for you change with the light glinting off the
windows of an anchored boat.
Mercury should be a young boy,
beautiful in his silver sandals. I see him
sailing his boat out of this bay.
I see how slender he is
how much younger than I, my son perhaps,
growing up silver-blond somewhere in California, also a Mercurial
figure, one that darts in and out of my brain,
slips out of my life like sand,
gives me the sense that nothing is stable,

nothing stands still long enough for savouring,
gives me what should turn into wisdom,
the sense that you cannot hold
or possess, but does not give me wisdom, gives me
longing
instead. Well, you are a September Mercury with Mercury in his silver
Ferrari, zooming over the hill on the Eastern horizon when you were
born, and he drives you everywhere you want to go now. Mercury
quickly vanishes when I look at him,
the silver disappears from my mirror, but that young blond lean
was walking, no, dancing over the hill in the East when I was born
too, and like a mirror catching the sun, like a
candle, led the moon into the first house where I lived.
And there are affinities, so let us not speak
of the movement. It doesn't stop.

Hard, cold, ambitious.
Are you all those things? If you
were, you would work harder and
play less.
Foolish, this attempting to account for everything which enters
our world. What is it that makes some of us keep
our feet on the brake
all the time, which makes us more dangerous than the uncautious
driver,
which ultimately leads to a failure of the brakes,
worn out
in that moment which becomes the head-on collision?

The birds provide easy metaphors.
Is there a bird who settles into the ground, digs in
and will not let go? A bird that doesn't like to
fly. One that does not move quickly?
One that changes infrequently?
One that lives a long and suffering life?
Surely, if there is, I am

that bird. No wings on my feet,
but I love those sweet-faced Mercuries.
An old man with beard and mustache tends my
life while I moon and lean towards those
silvery beach boys,
flesh waiting for its own silvery mirror image:
flesh, my son,
the young boy who wades into my dreams.

Thursday

This day I wake up
burned
bitten by insects
with a rash from some weed, proving
I am not a child of nature;
today I miss not only you,
to whom I address these notes, the young
old
Jupiter with the mustache. Today I miss myself,
a sense of life being real,
a sense of purpose.
I talked to you this evening,
by phone, realizing again I only love men I make up
in my head, wishing for your presence,
yet once more feeling that by word we do not communicate.
The you I want to speak to is a you
I never speak to, who perhaps
is not there to be spoken to.

So where are we in this imperfect world,
gluing our lives together with dream fibres,
depending on the dream code to send the
messages we need to hear?
The you I want to speak to
is in my head: but I cannot conjure him up

when you are gone.
See how our fantasies count on
reality? None of us
creates something which was never there before.
The question remains
how to deal with
what *is*
there.

Friday

Shall this be the day when Venus comes out of the foam?
I am leaving the waters
this morning,
going to see you,
though I do not say to anyone
this is my purpose in leaving.
I am ashamed perhaps
of trying so hard
to communicate with someone who does not want to hear.
At least not what I have to say,
a woman only,
one without an earth-shaking life.

Do you remember someone born
with a stone in his mouth? In my dream life I was born
with a snowflake on my tongue. It was a snowflake
carved from some soft creamy stone and when I
spoke it fell out of my mouth
and you picked it up and put it in your pocket.
In my dream you were made out of coffee
but the cream had all turned into
snowflakes.
I am travelling on a train made out of snowflakes.
Remember how fast snow-
flakes melt, and understand our speed.

40

Forgive me for addressing you
so personally.
The you I address melts as fast as a snowflake,
like talking to a burning coal,
imbuing the fire with life, as it has a life glowing in front of
you. How can I say I do not communicate with the fire?
It does not respond in my language;
neither do you.

Let me talk then;
it is my way of offering love.

Rescue Poem

When he diagnosed
my case,
it left me with little
hope.
"You have an invisible telephone booth
around you,"
he said.
"It is the glass hard cardamon whispers cannot penetrate.
Glass of cut-out tongues
and spider tracks,
of the turn of a bolt one thread
and of the distance one hammer-blow drives a nail.
The space of a snake's forehead
and the diamond ladder of a window washer.
A shadow foot between the real foot and the ground."

He smiles at my disease,
says he would like to put his arms around me
but cannot
reach around the whole invisible telephone
booth.
We walk through the night
trailing lizards.
Our heads are filled
with fat wet moss.
Black camels walk around
and through our eyes
stamping on the city streets.

We thread needles with our thin bones
and sew streets together
trying to hold them in finger pockets.

"I cannot get near you," he said. "That telephone booth
being in the way." In the way really
was the dial
tone—
the sound of ruby acorns pelting a roof of elbows.
"Busy, busy,"
the help signal gone crazy
reaching to years of hurricane weather.

Here are the tools to chop down an invisible telephone booth:
      an apple inside the ear
      a bucket of blood
      a hammer made out of beetle tongues
      a saw made from parts of the cheek
      teeth chipped out of the navel
      diamond breasts and a silver penis
Well, you came with strange luggage,
a man from your own trust company,
a bag full of incredible instruments. You looked at
the doctor and said,
"I'm a specialist. Is she
the one with the invisible telephone booth?
She the one nobody can get near?
She the one who stands naked inside it, making
long distance calls for help?
and has line-men out everyday wrecking
their instruments on this invisible glass?"

Yes, you had a bag with
      apples rolling inside your ears,
            shaking their seeds into Eustachian tubes
            and down alimentary canals,

buckets of blood were capped with silver
  fish skins and sloshed inside the black bag,
carrying hundreds of small initials,
your hammer of cricket tongues
        tapped itself to sleep
        waiting for the big job,
the saw made of all the soft parts of
  a cheek sharpened itself against eyebrows,
teeth chipped out of the navel were
        ready to bite
and diamond breasts with hard nipples
        rubbed against the silver penis
        causing the fish eyes to glow
You set to work at once
on the telephone booth.
            Need I say the obvious?
            That you found the door?
            That no one else had tried the obvious?
            Need I say more?
            An obvious solution to an obvious problem.
            Come in,
            Put in your silver nickel,
            your pennies,
            quarters,
            dimes.
            Come inside
            these invisible walls.

            Join me
            on the silver
            wirey
            inside.

Cerise

The color of dancing in plastic shoes
or carrying a plastic pocket book with cloth flowers showing thru
or gold speckled linoleum.

Come on, now. How can you take that color seriously?
Are you going to ask me to live with it on my bathroom mirror?
Why don't you put it on your teeth?
And smile with it?
And sell out
forever; you've lost me. Talking "kultur" but not liking it.
Putting down the modern, but liking it.
Where are the traditional bones in your body? Where are
the primary colors? And where
can I find a bird other than a parakeet in your house?
those itsy, bitsies.

Well, I might as well say this now. There are
so many differences between us. It's not just a difference of
years, a generation perhaps,
but of values, life-style, maybe, and mostly everything deep inside.
And your love of that color—cerise—
epitomizes it all.

A Japanese parasol:
maybe I can take a cerise Japanese parasol,
but not for the rain.

Get me back to old wood,
to reading books rather than talking about them,
to telling stories and listening to sounds rather than mocking them,
to primary colors,
to accepting the old and the new but not like a sponge,
and not spewing it out like a welding torch showering
its pseudo-hot sparks along the scaffolding.

Oh, am I getting so old?
You look to drugs to show you colors when the colors are there all
the time and you can see them, you could see them, you will
see them at will
yes, at will,
any time you want them
not chemically
but biochemically;
protesting a war—yet willing to beat up somebody who steals
your girl.
False values somewhere? or a misassessment?

I am not protesting a color.
Some dawn
everybody's bound to get up just once
and see the sun rise and just that
peculiar cerise will seep over the sky
making neon signs look ugly and dirty.
I'm not saying cerise is no good.
But you made me mad. You make me mad. All of you, all of you who
are so cocky you won't listen to new things and old things
or really anything at all,
but most of all you make me mad. All of you
who won't tolerate the existence of anything
but yourselves.

Paint everything cerise,
if that is the color you currently like.

46

Paint me cerise. and my walls, and my friends, and my books,
and my brain, and my street, and my town, and my state, and
my country, and my flag, and any means of transportation I have
of getting out of it all.
Leave me alone.
LEAVE ME ALONE.
I don't want to be cerise today.
I don't like cerise today.
Cerise is the color of discotheques today
and today I'm not ready for discotheques
or you
or even your bloody cerise.

Just keep your paint brush and
your spray can to yourself.
Let me go back to my primary colors for a while;
isn't there room for more than one color in this world?
Be careful of the man who likes cerise.
He wraps himself up in his flag at night,
wounding the red until it bleeds cerise,
and picking the stars off
so they won't stick in his mustache.
He dances.
He dances. Away from my house. He leaves my house free of cerise
for a few hours. I breathe a sigh of relief, open the windows
and go back to red, white, and blue.

And I turn on Beethoven,
a symphony,
very loud.

This Beautiful Black Marriage

Photograph negative
her black arm: a diving porpoise,
sprawled across the ice-banked pillow.
Head: a sheet of falling water.
Her legs: icicle branches breaking into light.

This woman,
photographed sleeping.
The man,
making the photograph in the acid pan of his brain.
Sleep stain them both,
as if cloudy semen
rubbed shiningly over the surface
will be used to develop their images.

       on the desert
       the porpoises curl up,
       their skeleton teeth are bared by
       parched lips;
       her sleeping feet
       trod on scarabs,
       holding the names of the dead
       tight in the steady breathing.

       This man and woman have married
       and travel reciting
       chanting
       names of missing objects.

They enter a pyramid.
A black butterfly covers the doorway
like a cobweb,
folds around her body,
the snake of its body
closing her lips.
her breasts are stone stairs.
She calls the name, "Isis,"
and waits for the white face to appear.

No one walks in these pyramids at night.
No one walks during
the day.
You walk in that negative time,
the woman's presence filling up the space
as if she were incense; man walks
down the crevices and
hills of her body.
Sounds of the black marriage
are ritual sounds.
Of the porpoises dying on the desert.
The butterfly curtaining the body,
The snake filling the mouth.
The sounds of all the parts coming together
in this one place,
the desert pyramid,
built with the clean historical
ugliness of men dying at work.

If you imagine, friend, that I do not have those
black serpents in the pit of my body,
that I am not crushed in fragments by the tough butterfly wing
broken and crumpled like a black silk stocking,
if you imagine that my body is not
blackened

burned wood,
then you imagine a false woman.

This marriage could not change me.
Could not change my life.
Nor is it that different from any other marriage.
They are all filled with desert journeys,
with Isis who holds us in her terror,
with Horus who will not let us see
the parts of his body joined
but must make us witness them in dark corners,
in bloody confusion;
and yet this black marriage,
as you call it,
has its own beauty.
As the black cat with its rich fur
stretched and gliding smoothly down the tree trunks.
Or the shining black obsidian
pulled out of mines and polished to the cat's eye.
Black as the neat seeds of a watermelon,
or a pool of oil, prisming the light.
Do not despair this "black marriage."
You must let the darkness out of your own body; acknowledge it
and let it enter your mouth,
taste the historical darkness openly.
Taste your own beautiful death,
see your own photo image,
as x-ray,
bone bleaching inside the blackening
flesh

Filling the Boxes of Joseph Cornell

Aren't we nasty little people
looking at treasure boxes?
          here is one having a pair of chocolate legs
          in high heels,
          a silver mirror,
          a beef tongue, slightly purplish
          and streaked, like meat turning bad,
and only wanting to
change their contents;
fill them with ourselves?

          The structure of anger
          is repetition;
          tell him over and over you saw the girl he raped
          and killed, her face streaked purple
          large blotches on her breasts,
          part of the hand severed
          and thrown across the room,
          and over and over you tell him
          yelling at him about how you saw her and what he
          did, and how you hate him and how he took someone's
          life, and the structure of your anger
          is *only* repetition,
          of all the ugly things,
          over and over . . .

               (I'll say, "he hurt me,
               he hurt me,"

over and over,
thinking about the assault,
trying to make it go away
out of my head
all memory of him leave me.

we are standing outside of a window displaying
electronic equipment. $100 for this small speaker,
$300 for this turn table. $400 for this amplifier.
You can scarcely contain yourself, wanting all these beautiful
square boxlike parts that will make sounds slip into your
ears like a beautiful pair of hands.

When I used to go to the movies on Friday nights with my
mother and sister in Whittier, California, we used to see the
previews of coming attractions, and even though I knew
that we went to the movies every week-end, I
could scarcely sit in my seat,
wanting so physically to be there, seeing the new movie
in color perhaps with Betty Grable wearing chocolate colored
stockings and sitting in her dressing room looking at
the mirror, while the rich ugly man
brought her flowers and the poor handsome
man waited outside.

Whose tongue was hanging out for her?

Your tongue hanging out for new hi-fi equipment.
No matter where we see the scenes, we are structuring
the parts we like, putting them into little stagelike boxes
of our own, with our own additions—
        some ostrich feathers,
        a silver inkwell,
        a dime bank, a photo of a countess,
        a graduation certificate;

fill them ourselves, as if the world had no artistry,
no sense of placement, no choice
settling things where they were settled.

> The old man, my kind father-in-law,
> saying after having painted watercolors for 20 years,
> little landscapes and vases of flowers,
> getting up at 5 in the morning to go into the city
> and sketch for an hour before work
> and whose only problem was that he had little talent—
> though skill was something he knew about
> and tried to perfect—
> he said, as we drove through the country,
> that he always changes the landscape when he paints it,
> because there is no good arrangement in nature,
> only he always changed it
> by putting in the same barn,
> the same two rocks,
> and the same boat, even when there was no water,
> the boat then being disguised as a bush

Aren't we nasty little people,
looking at boxes, never accepting what is there,
always putting in our own arrangements?

> The structure of anger
> is repetition. We are angered by people trying to
> arrange our lives for us—no structure we
> build being suitable for all others,
> the argument about whether this war is worse than
> all other wars—two pacifists militantly fighting about
> when it's right to kill, another pacifist
> saying how killing can only be evil,
> but letting his parents destroy him, kill him
> with softness and tenderness and kindness
> at an early age, and how he doing it to his own child,
> and she in anger, even as a 10-year-old, lashing

out in anger, not learning to read, not learning to
talk, not learning to keep herself clean, and secretly
knowing what she is doing,
killing,
this repetition, over and over

The same poem, the same life, the same destructive relationships,
relating the color—if it's blue
        I   am blue
        I am blue as a blues singer
        I am blue in the face from saying the same things
            over & over
        I am blue because of you and what you've done to me
        I am blue because it was my favorite color as a baby
        (it didn't take much to teach me
        that my parents wanted a boy
        and the best adjustment I could make was to
        like blue)

Little boy blue, come blow your horn
Sheep's in the meadow, cow's in the corn.

Repetition is the structure of anger.

You keep saying something over and over
and it goes away
or you go away from it,
ultimately being bored with too much of a good thing.

There is a man who keeps making boxes
and putting new and strange and beautiful things in them.
        a map of all the currents of all the oceans in the world
        and a silver instrument of steering a ship
        sometimes lady's objects; sometimes men's.
        Never the same; never a repetition of subject,
        but always the box, over and over.

Repetition is what structures our lives . . . Where we find a unity
we find a work of art, some sense,
something we call a life?

For years I have been repeating formulae I learned to
keep my devils away; and now I don't have any devils, but I say
the same formulae when angels are around
and
of course
they go away too.

The structure of repetition is one that makes songs
and dances and boxes
            I don't want to repeat myself.
            It seems to be the only way of getting a point across
            though

Across the ocean I know someone who's repeating himself
and who repeated himself
            just as when someone doesn't hear you, they will
            ask you to repeat what you said,
            or there might to be a repeat broadcast of something we liked
            on the radio, or you might have to repeat a course you
            failed in school or when you belch you are
            repeating your food.
            Mainly,
            repetition is for learning or for fear

Have I repeated myself enough? Little boy blue,
that's you.
I never turned out to be Little Boy Blue,
just a woman who likes blue a lot,
even the blues,
If I repeat your name three hundred times in a row
it will begin to sound absurd;
if I replayed our life together, all the scenes three hundred

times they too would seem absurd—but everything in the world
would, under such conditions

What I want most of all is to repeat your name
until you become something real,
not a fantasy.
What I want is a structure of repetition
that makes me angry,
makes me strong
(because, as Martha said, anger is a stronger emotion
in our culture).
For once,
I'd like to look at the artist's velvet-lined box
and enjoy his world.
My tongue is not large and purple and streaked with rot,
as his beef tongue.
Mine has smaller,
different things to say.

It is a mark of determination
or stupidity
to repeat your mistakes.

A Room Away from You

the mirror
            "when I look into your eyes,"
                you said,
            "I see only myself."
the mirror here reflects
milk weed pods, like exploded feathers, the brown seed
with little whorls, as a fingertip,
the mirror's surface, seemingly smoked

perhaps you spoke of me, 2000 miles away, and the air
made these strange caterpillars and
buds of smoke forming a film,
veiling the brown wings of my hair,
also reflected, coming together,
via wind, or maybe even
the seed pods having blown from where
you are.

the window on the bird papered wall
            the dancer, in her interview, said,
            "I held a bird in my mouth
                because I wanted to give the image of me
                holding a bird in my mouth."
the feet on the lips
thin tracks,
perhaps like a few hair pins held on the lip,
the bird's warm round body pressed between the teeth,
a pulse, fast beating which you could feel if you put your
hand on my breast,

or perhaps the breast of another woman,
as you are now doing,
but, in the bird,
held between the dancer's lips,
not quite knowing what she is saying to the world,
having divorced her husband
and I,
the never dancer
who wants to move, as water, in the world,
sitting here
a heavy calm body
remembering the times you lifted me and danced me
like a child
around the room.
It hurt under my arms,
and I felt heavy
and very close to you.

That's what I can't get used to . . .
being, feeling, so close
and then not being together at all,
    biting my words, like fingernails, that don't give me
    the comfort of your arms.

    and the window looks out on a scene
    where I can't see you.

the sketch
you told me I didn't know what it was like to be alone.

and I remembered once
saying that
to somebody else.

a sketch drawn finer
than the veins
in an azalea petal
of a girl and boy,

trying to find the place on the bark of the tree
where a name was carved
and with it a sign saying, "BE AS SILENT AS POSSIBLE"

the silence in our heads

conducting to a house filled with the white-sheeted spirits
of all our friends, telling us
about the next stage of life, when we all become
trees. I want to tell you how
long I stood alone.

I was a Silver Weeping Birch
bare in winter
and silvery green in spring
and no finger had this ring on it,
a piece of metal you tried to take away from me,
but each finger had to reach down to the earth
to try to touch something
alone
no place to move,
the illusion of movement when the wind blew,
but never moving from that spot

      the fingers only grow down, and move, as in water,
with the wind, touch no one who doesn't touch them.

Being alone is being
a tree.
Your roots eating the thick black dirt
and your trunk not moving even when words are carved on it
with a penknife.

I am in a room away from you.
Right now, I am alone.

III

From The Tarot Deck

The Empress

If she were
arrested
in the middle
of
thought
      her mind—
      a crystal wafer,
      the lens so small it could be lost in the
      cat's fur
might crack
or
be scratched.

Leave
each process
Let
it unfold.
      A bud,
      her breast.
      An acorn,
      underneath.
One day you found the corn
with its new shoot
exposed.

One day
in the winter.

I would think it
an accident.
Still,
I would say,
it doesn't matter.

The Empress No. 5

She took the bone from her arm.
This music frenzied the wild gazelles
and the milk pigs running
under the high arches of her feet
and past her heavy black-budded breasts.
Taking this instrument
to / file / the words / in her
shawl, spilling
out in dis-
order, honing each
syllable
till the screeching
became a har-
mony, till the buzz
became small on the smooth edge
of a word,
she set herself
a simple task. But the music in her own
armbone was so loud / she set /
the thicket / within her
running. Arm bone. Arm bone. Arm bone.
The arm bone sings. The arm bone sings.
And the gazelles leap under her armpits.
The small pigs snuffle and run past
lips. The birds caw, caw.
What noise / as she only makes / a word.
Commotion for
every syllable

The Hermit

With gravel glued together for arms and legs,
charcoal-blackened wood for feet,
hands,
the body a leather bolster,
head a hard ball—
            the withered dried up man who had
            eaten nothing but sweetened dew for 30 years
            knelt by the roadside.
            A robber attacked him from behind
            cutting down the old man with his knife.
            He put on the old man's ragged robe
            and himself began to pray.
            "Lord, Lord, I have killed a good man
            gratuitously. What shall I do?"
            But nothing happened.
            The old man's body began to rot.
            The robber sang and chanted.
            He forgot
            after some time
            his origins.

Sun

Under my elbow. In my elbow.
Under my bed. In my bed.
Under my foot. In my foot.
Under my eye. In my eye.

       Yes. Yes. I've found it.
The lost key, key, key, key, key, key—
What bird sings that song
       Key, key

A bird made out of keys,
flying to unlock the sun. let out the heat.
flying to unlock the moon. and let out the milk.
flying to unravel the mountain.
and resting on a branch saying,
key, key.

King of Pentacles:
This Figure Has No Special Description

The bull's head is all skull;
the hide wrapped round
the bones like a web;
the eyes glazed
like fruits.
It is a symbol,
like John the Baptist's head, on
a tray.

* * *

One night you gave me the ultimatum.
You said, "I'm leaving for Texas in my jaguar."
You said, "I'm not taking you with me
because you can't drive a car,
ride a horse,
and you only wear a size 32 brassiere."
My feelings snapped like a glass pipette,
and I got out my cards.
They said the King of Pentacles has
bulls' heads on his throne
and thick bunches of red grapes on his
robe.
The bull takes the grapes in his mouth,
crushes them
stem and all
and stains the throne a deep mauve.

* * *

In Texas there is a thunderstorm.
The clouds are like heavy clusters
of wine sediment.
The rain pours down and it is beaujolais.
In Texas you are wrangling horses when the wine-rain starts.
Your jaguar has broken from the muzzle of the car and turned wild,
so your only means of transportation now
is horse.
In Texas
no woman wears a size 32 brassiere,
and they all ride horses,
or drive cars.
But you have found the land too dry and dusty
for your liking
and are thinking of travelling on to Mexico where they put hot
peppers in all their food.

* * *

At home I sit with my hands on the cards.
I marvel at the yellow sky.
I cope with all negative emotions in diamond-hard resiliency:
the cards
flat surfaces
slick
and cold to the touch.
But what happens when
my body softens
to,
say,
love and the diamond edges
become pools?
The bull's skull,
the bull's eye—you;
the tongue of the bull
rough

but warm all over my body
like a towel.
How do I cope with my feelings
when you deliver your ultimatum and drive off to Texas in your jaguar?
The pools run dry—are sucked up by the sand.
The diamonds lie at the bottom,
like dull salt crystals.
The skull lying in the desert feels
the skin thinning
and tightening into a web
before it breaks away—
dried into nothing.
The eyes—
the bull's eyes—
are empty sockets.
My body dries out
and becomes a bone sceptre
with which you reign, King of Pentacles,
from your throne.

3 of Swords
—for dark men under the white moon

Yes,
of old wire hangers that remain in the closet,
of the Satsuma plum tree you crawled out of the window to
        (in the dark
        after they thought their ten-year-old child was asleep
        but was
        resting in the branches
        like a cat who knows where to sit himself
        silkily
        down
        resting surrounded by leaves
        rustling like many hands dealing cards swiftly)
Yes,
of the moon in her wet menstrual period
lacing rust streaks across a crater,
of the dust in the old lady's hairnet,
of running the greyhound in the closet where he can only move
½ of a leap,
of grubby fingers shooting the white aggie,
of a pot of soup on a cold night—
        pictures of . . .
        in the moon's bloodshot eye;
        your sleep is ghost sleep.
        No wonder you are always tired;
        you run
        the coyote with his ragged smelly hunger
        in my dreams every night.

I watch you
pacing
in the rim of the hills
I watch you
stealing
delicately
even from the bullet-marked foot.

Asters grow in the backyard,
some under your bed.
What we never speak of is that
I love too many men
and would not be unfaithful to myself.
I am the sword with
the starry hilt.
Dream of me. I love you in a rain of grey paint
as I love the coyote for his stealing
and the lonely Westerner for his silver bullets,
and all George Washingtons—1st and last—
and the men who hold out that wild card
—the three of swords—
not knowing
my heart melts and bleeds and runs
for their steel;
it sings for piercing
and it accepts hungrily the knife;
it comes for its exercise in a bed made
of swords
and asks, genuinely, to be rebathed
in thick plasma each night.

How can I tell you
the moon was made to shine alone each night
walking to her bath and undressing alone.
Her breasts spout milk
and her children slide down from the sky.

Her lovers she nibbles and whispers to,
sends messages by the wind to touch their ears,
takes, allows herself to be taken calmly
each day
away.

Oh how can I tell you, she loves you,
but wants to be alone,
wants to be in your wrist,
a pulse,
but not in your house. See,
she is outside the window now.
You look at her.
It does not mean you should try
to bring her inside.

Six of Cups

If you spin me around until I'm so dizzy
I'm a blue top,
there is no reason to believe I will
have lost my sense of direction
when I stop.
I simply will not have the heart to go on.

POEM FOR A CARD

Pretend means something different every time.
The two children gathering flowers
in the high walled garden,
filling their cups with blossoms,
must see that there is a star,
white-hot, as it fell from the sky, burning its way down
on top of each receptacle,
but they do not seem to be aware that it changes the contents
in any way.
They hand each other the cups;
perhaps they touch the stars floating on top
as if they were hot cookies
or pieces of gingerbread fresh from the oven.
The cups are toys that they hand one another for examination
and sampling—proud of ownership,
proud of each pretty star.
If I put my hand on one of their stars,
my hand would disintegrate into a lump of carbon in a minute,
without even a chance for me to reflect and draw back.

I have to keep my hand away from that ten-thousand-degree star.
But still they hand each other the cups,
smiling and bowing,
presenting for love
something I do not need them to tell me the value of.
They could as well hand me the cup
with a coral snake inside
curled up like a carved face.

POEM AFTER THE CARD

Do not tell me that when I am sterile I should quit trying to pro-
duce. If you were once jealous because I seemed to have so much,
you are now jealous that I have so little. What is it?
Do you want to own me?
Do you want both my former fullness and now my present emptiness?
Do you want to take my memories and make them your memories?
Do you want to take my hand, cut it off, and say it is your hand?
Don't you know I brought the desert with me
and that you can't live in it?
I still have those three oranges I bought at the roadside stand.
I know those birds are going to fly out of them, sure as anything—
and you know it too.
So what are you hanging around for?
You want me to give you an orange?
You know that bird's going to be in it.
You just don't seem to know when to stop.
You'll die in this desert.
It's all the same to me, but don't you care?
I have my own reasons for being here,
but by now you should know they're crazy ones.
Do you really think you'll stick around till I die,
like some old man hanging around an old miser till he dies,
hoping to find out where he's hiding his gold?
Man, you're going to be disappointed.
When you find my cache, it's just going to be sticks.

Bare sticks,
and those oranges—by now they don't even have birds in them.
Don't you understand? I have nothing.
Can't you leave me alone to die in my own cactus,
my own sun, my own thirst?
You can't even stand that I have that, can you?
Stop walking on my shadow. You'll wear it out.
If you must be on me all the time, at least
put only your shadow,
not your body,
on my shadow. The weight is almost unbearable.

POEM ON THE CARD

We almost made it with our stars and fruit, didn't we?
Pretending we could get away from the truth even for a minute.
Pretending we could talk about objects rather than events,
as if objects were even real,
as if there were such a thing as being concrete
I guess we knew we'd never make it,
all along.
I guess being little and playing with cups heaped with flowers and
stars is what we wished our past were.
I guess having that orange with a bird in it really sounded
more like what we wanted than having an orange with juice in it.
I guess we want to think that being honest is saying the truth
so that it sounds like we understand it.
I guess we want to give everything grace,
make everything clean.
I guess we want the illusion of what we want more
than what we want
because we think we are wise and know
it's harder to destroy an illusion
than what the illusion stands for:
the star, burning the flowers in those gold cups,
held and exchanged by the children.

Looking for the Sign on Fulham Road
(The Star)

A sign, a portent,
it could be
the name: Plumtree Court
where I expect to see trees with narrow green leaves like
bus tickets or caterpillars shading small purple
plums.
But there are only bricks.
It could be a shop called, "Dreamware"
and I expect to see sleep masks covered with large paste diamonds
or ivory satin sheets, perhaps a special set of earphones
to pipe poetry or songs into your ear while sleeping
or special scented pillowcases, some smelling like cinnamon,
some like musk, others like fat climbing roses.
But they sell common nightwear.

Could the sign be a long dirty feather from a pheasant
which was lying at the steps of the labor ministry building?
or the small card saying, "Maureen Morgan" and "December 23, 1965"?
There were two in the gutter.

In the window of "Hart & Son" butcher, there were dressed
turkeys and game cocks, full pigs, one without a head.
No, that was not the sign. How could a man
named Hart be in the butchering business?
And in a nearby window there was a large basket of goose eggs.
Does this mean that my trip
on this day of waiting

was a goose egg
a zero
a nothing
a day without signs?

There were no book stalls where I could find Hermetic
literature, though a paper I've never heard of
called *The Morning Star* was housed on this street.
What is the morning star, and why does it shine when the other
meteors have fallen on the road?

What is the sign
I was to have received on this road
today?
Was it
the story of Anna's ghost?
coming to her room that night when she was 16
having spent the summer sailing so that her body was brown,
old Katherine coming to her room to say,
"The gloves you bought me were too small,"
her voice glimmering like the mist with its Irish accent
the wooden chest behind her, solidly,
still holding in a small drawer the gloves which Anna had come back
too late to give.

The sign must come like dawn. You cannot see its
arrival, but know when it is there.
Just as the Crimson Ibis gets its color from eating certain shrimps
and marine life, so the sign changes the one who
receives it. I dip my fingers into a basin of water,
and see the moon reflected,
or is it a stone, or a fish,
flashing away to a darker pool?

IV

The Ice Eagle

The Canoer

the hush of
the river
at 4 a.m.,
fish flipper their bellies across moss,
trees walk down to the very shoreline
thinking nobody is watching them,
his paddle darts in and out of
the water, getting better acquainted
each time with its own slippery
texture,
hands boggle out of the river
offering foam money in the corner of his eye.

In my own mind
I change the texture of the river,
super-imposing on it
a buffalo, bleeding in the hindquarters,
not raging but calm and taking
the waters. The river dries up
around him, and the skeleton of the buffalo
walks down the dried-out bed of an old river.

Ringless

I cannot stand the man who wears
a ring
on his little finger/ a white peacock walking on the moon
and splinters of silver dust his body;
but the great man, George, cracked in half in my living room
one day and I saw he was made of marble
with black veins. It does not justify the ring to say
someone gave it to you and the little finger is the only one
it will fit;
it does not justify to say Cocteau wore one
and still made the man burst silently through the mirror—
many beautiful
poems have been made with rings worn on the little finger.
That
isn't the point.
Flaubert had jasper; Lorca had jade; Dante had
amber; and Browning had carnelian;
George Washington had solid gold—even Kelly once wore a scarab there;
but I am telling you I cannot stand the man
who wears a ring
on his little finger. He may indeed
run the world;
that does not make him any better in
my needlepoint eyes.
Why
is a story.

>   There were heaps of fish lying, shimmering in the sun
>   with red gashes still heaving

and the mouths of medieval lovers.
There were gold and green glass balls bobbing in their
nets on the waves.
There were black-eyed men with hair all over their bodies
There were black-skirted ladies baking bread
and there were gallons and gallons of red wine.
A girl spilled one drop of hot wax on her lover's neck
as she glanced at his white teeth and thick arms.
There were red and silver snakes coiling around the legs
of the dancers.
There was hot sun and there was no talk.
How do I reconcile these images with our cool president,
George Washington, walking the streets? Every bone
in my body is ivory and has the word, "America"
carved on it, but
my head takes me away from furniture and pewter
to the sun tugging at my nipples and trying to squeeze
under my toes.
The sun appeared in the shape of a man and he had
a ring made of sun around his little finger.
"It will burn up your hand," I said.
But he made motions in the air and passed by.
The moon appeared in the shape of a young negro boy,
and he had a ring made of dew around his little finger.
"You'll lose it," I said,
but he touched my face,
not losing a drop and passed away. Then I saw
Alexander Hamilton, whom I loved,
and he had a ring on his little finger,
but he wouldn't touch me.
And Lorca had rings around both little fingers,
and suddenly everyone I knew appeared,
and they all had rings on their little fingers,
and I was the only one in the world left without any
rings
on any

of my fingers whatsoever.
And worst of all,
there was George Washington
walking down the senate aisles
with a ring on his little finger—managing
the world,
managing *my* world.
This is what I mean—you wear a ring on your
          little finger
          and you manage the world,
          and I am ringless
          ringless . . .
I cannot stand the man who wears
a ring
on his little finger;

not even if it is you.

The Blackbird

The wind is a blackbird.
I am a blackbird.
When you watch a blackbird
flying down-wind
you
cannot tell
if the wind is really the wind
or the bird is a bird.

You cannot know
how to listen,
but if you listen
you can tell.

The wind and the blackbird
do not sound
the same.

An Apology

Past exchanges have left orbits of rain around my face,
Words used-up as the empty shell of the beetle.
      I did not mean to insult you,
      but perhaps wanted to scorch you with that steamy teakettle
      of my 2700 years,
      to tell you youth shouldn't be humble as the tablecloth,
      but arrogant and fierce/
      we get toothless with age;
      should bite hard when we're young.
      To tell you not to follow masters whose egos are sponges,
      To tell you not that you had nothing to say
      but that you need to pour it out at you own speed,
      in an empty space where it will knock against you.
      I saw the dream of the tongue floating in a bowl of water
      as a desperate sacrifice. You,
      giving up your own words,
      You, giving up identity to float safely on display in
      another man's ocean;
      I saw everything that made me weep spools of rotten thread
      for my own disconnected life—
      drop cement trowels from my knees and
      broken clocks from my elbows.
      Wanting to discard the past; renege my own life, the pain
      of recognition and hate mingles with the identity.
      I apologize for lack of grace—
      not passing you with a zen stance.
      Elders should be lacquered in their place.
      And women commit their words

to the dream code; toads & shooting stars in the blood,
icy milk pails,
snow,
oranges,
diamonds, eyes to the ground. Women should be
silently riding their zebras.

Slicing Oranges for Jeremiah

as the juice ran out on the wooden board
      the third orange you had cut for this son of yours
      opened
      and he grabbed the slices like a little raccoon running to
      prepare them,
      carrying his bowl to the table where he ate,
his instinct trying to make up for something not in his throat
or his fingers,
trying to make up for the thyroid gland he was born without
      he would eat a dozen oranges if you would let him
rosy Jeremiah, with long eyelashes

what does it mean
if a child cannot talk when he is six,
if he shits in the toilet one day; in his pants the next?
what does it mean
if a man drinks and can't earn enough money?
and what if he tells his wife he'd like another woman
but wouldn't have one,
and what does it mean
if he tells his wife she's unpleasant or dull
and what
does
it mean
if his wife takes sleeping pills or walks
in front of a car?
and what
does it mean,

if Jeremiah takes the sun
and slices it up
like the oranges and eats a little fire
thirsty for the juice?

When you take the knife in your hand
to slice an orange first into quarters, then into eighths,
each slice shining—
              as orange jelly, a goldfish,
              lights on the water at night,
and you cut, competently, efficiently, a housewife
who knows how to divide,
when you take your instrument and use it
making pools of orange juice, letting the peel spray into
your nostrils,
what does it mean?
                        And your son,
eating orange after orange,
until I felt the juice in my own mouth,
just watching,
and the sweetness,
and I wondered what was missing,
or why,
and where his thyroid went
or why there was no gland there,
and how even this baby animal,
your son,
must know that it was you who kept him alive,
remembering his pill each day,
and taking him places where people would respect him
and letting him make drawings
and build garbage structures:
and how his father knew too
it was you who kept him, your husband, alive,
giving him whatever artificial gland it was you did each day,
and how they both resented it,

depending on it as they did,
the men needing the woman more than any man could admit.

And what does it mean,
this strength you have?
It keeps you hovering towards death.
It keeps you near the pill bottles and close to the wheels of cars.
It keeps you sad and compassionate,
willing to understand the miseries of others.
It isn't weakness that points us towards death,
but strength, men dying earlier than women,
trying to show their strength,
women taking their own lives with gas, in ovens with their
gold-clock babies under their aprons,
with sleeping pills glistening like amber necklaces poured into
the stomach's cave,
stepping quietly under car wheels,
as they lie with their men at night,
not murmuring,
enduring
until the breath is pushed out.

Slicing oranges for your son,
you cannot see what I see,
the oranges growing outside my own back door when I was five,
the dusty dark citrus leaves making black smudges
against my sweater.
There is a gypsy in me
who wants to run
with all these oranges in a bag
and trade them for the sun
or find someone who will cut them for me
the way you slice them for Jeremiah.
That care;
that efficiency.
Instead of some gland, I might have

an orange tree
growing just behind my throat
straining to stay alive, to endure,
waiting for the efficient hand to reach inside
and slice the oranges
as you do,
as I saw you
slice oranges for Jeremiah,
slice the oranges for your son
who could eat a dozen you said
if you'd let him.

Summer

he slid out of the skin, leaving it
like a dried lima bean hull,
white and papery on the road.
his body inched along
the highway,
rippling its new red colors
bits of brown
like stones
seemed strewn along each arm and thigh.
it was a strange transformation
which had been coming.
the moon had warned him flipping like a fish in the sky,
a bowl of sweet cream left overnight emptied itself to the snake
living under the hearth.
when the time had come the old skin had shucked off
crackling. no pain
no pulling. he slid his wet body into the sun,
he was dry now
and brown.
the ocean rushed through his head; he heard the crabs
moving sideways on the bottom
and the fish
shouting
with their fins.

The Ice Eagle

It was with resolution that she gave up the
powerful teardrops in her eyes—
that crystal, the Venus-soft lizard-eyed creature called woman, gazes
through, her philosopher's stone,
the sweet glass
that drops from the sky.
Ancients,
in sacrifice,
cut off tears
with knives.

* * *

The 50 lb. eagle carved out of ice
sitting in the silver punch bowl
turned her attention to physical details.
            Why am I saying
            "her"?
            It is I,
            undoubtedly I,
            the life a dream work.
Undoubtedly the life has been confused with the movies,
I, Gloria Swanson, walking discontented
for all parties become that to me. I cannot
walk through the rituals
without my golden mask,
alas, 3 dozen of them hang on my wall,
the thick lips reminding me of what has been eaten
and has not nourished.

Physical details: the lawn that sloped down to the sea cliffs,
the swallows building their nests in rafters,
the stone house punctured with courts and patios,
Bougainvillea winding up its sides,
raw old Spanish wood composing chests and high still chairs
moved and touched into water-like smoothness,
the gravel driveway balancing the cutaway heels
of beautiful women,
the men swimming through the night in dinner jackets like papercups
floating on the ocean;
yes, her eyes—
        again why do I say
        "her",
        I must insist it is I.
my eyes are informed of silk and the obsidian minds of the rich.
Here is a thick glossy black smooth idea—sex and nothing else.
The rich are born bored
and look for purposes, causes, projects
to keep them busy.
The women make up wild malachite eyes, green with beautiful
sleep and restless knowledge of new plays,
new dancers,
new books,
new jazz. They
can ring their Egyptian eyes with kohl
and be aesthetes
and in veils walk down the rock path to the sea;
riding black tigers of Sartre and Camus and Ionesco,
yards of chiffon trailing their heels and they despair
the men,
they, I, we
        all women when it gets past social class
despair the men who have only the moon in their milky fluid fingers.
Yes, they wait,
the sun god we wait,

to find him naked in a blaze of fire.
We are stuck with vulgar substitutes—
the fashionable avant-garde dancer,
the sensational beat poet,
the jazz trumpeter,
the negro novelist,
and Amen-ra, Amen-ra, our father, they are all glorious sun-brilliant
artists, but
homosexuals
fucking each other, riding on their own black panthers
wading into the iron waters.
Again the women must rest their bodies against each other and moan.
It is not the mysteries that draw the men,
but the fear of that great mystery
the veiled woman, Isis,
mother, whom they fear to be greater than all else.

And I am sick unto death. Sick,
I say, sick. We live in a world where men have forgotten their offices
only taking the woman
            like good debaters
            assigned to the positive side
            on whom rests the burden of
            proof
only taking her on the surface—
she, I, we, can peel off layer after layer where you
have taken her and yet find the bottom deep and tight and untouched
and longing for the greater measure.

She, no it was I, walked with the moon in Pisces,
and felt the trout slipping down into the ocean.
The carved ice eagle of that party
was melting
into the gin and strawberries.
In its beak
someone had placed an American flag.

I found it hard to believe myself in this slippery unreal
man-made country. Look, look, look
I want to say; the eagle is a powerful bird.
In your fear, all you can do is carve him out of ice.
And that leaves only one alternative
in this temperate climate.
The ice eagle can do nothing
but melt.